This Is My Story To Tell

Set In Soul

© 2020 Tatiana Media LLC in partnership with Set In Soul LLC

ISBN #: 978-1-949874-86-0

Published by Tatiana Media LLC

All rights reserved. No part of this journal/publication may be reproduced, stored in a retrieval system, or transmitted in any form or by any means, electronic, mechanical, photocopying, recording, scanning, or otherwise, except as permitted under Section 107 or 108 of the 1976 United States Copyright Act whatsoever without express written permission from the author, except in the case of brief quotations embodied in critical articles and reviews. Please refer all pertinent questions to the publisher.

Limit of Liability/Disclaimer of Warranty: While the publisher and author have used their best efforts in preparing this book/journal, they make no representations or warranties with respect to the accuracy or completeness of the contents of this book/journal and specifically disclaim any implied warranties. The advice and strategies contained herein may not be suitable for your situation. You should consult with a professional where appropriate. Neither the publisher nor author shall be liable for any loss of profit or any other emotional, physical, spiritual and mental distress and damages, including but not limited to special, incidental, consequential, or other damages.

For general information on our other products and services, please contact our Customer Support within the United States at support@setinsoul.com.

Tatiana Media LLC as well as Set In Soul LLC publishes its books in a variety of electronic formats. Some content that appears in print may not be available in electronic books.

This Journal Belongs To

_____

**Dedicated To Me.
Growing And Healing.**

Table Of Contents

How To Use This Journal	6
What Is Domestic Abuse?	7
Signs Of Domestic Abuse	10
Opening Up	13
Leaving Safely	40
When I Left	42
Doing This For Me: Daily Healing	44

How To Use This Journal

Domestic abuse is defined as a pattern of threatening, violent, coercive, and degrading behavior and incidents that can include sexual violence by a partner or member of the family. Domestic abuse often displays itself through verbal assault, threats, and then violence. While physical injury is said to be the most obvious signs of danger, psychological and emotional bruises are also characteristics of domestic abuse that have great impacts to one's overall wellness. Experiencing this form of abuse can cripple your self-esteem and give you a false negative image towards yourself. It's time to stick up for yourself by writing down all that you have gone through. Though writing you can create your future and fill it with love while building and living presently in hope. Create a plan of action while having a place to express yourself daily and safely.

This journal is created to be your best friend through this time in your life. This is where you can be free, open and honest with yourself. It is here where you can define what it is that you want and define what it is that you no longer want. It is also here where you have a voice that no one can silence. We understand that this season may be difficult for you but just remember that there are still other seasons to look forward to. So begin by writing down your experiences no matter how bad they are. You are on the road to healing. Acknowledging that something happened and then accepting what happened and lastly recognizing how damaging it is/was to you and others around you is the first step to releasing. By filling out this journal you will start to build confidence towards yourself that is real even when you are alone and not a false sense of who you are supposed to be. The things that you have silenced within yourself to cover up for your abuser can now freely be let out here. We recommend filling out this journal every morning to rewire your mind and create an internal space where you feel love, safe and protected. This is a space where you can dwell with God. As soon as you start realizing your value, you will start taking actions that support that. You have started by already receiving this journal so it's now time to dedicate this moment to rebuilding you. Whether you are currently in a domestic abusive relationship or recently out of one, this journal is here to serve you and be a place to tell your story. Let's get start.

What Is Domestic Abuse?

What I Believe Domestic Abuse Is....

The Actual Definition Of Domestic Abuse....

Signs Of Domestic Abuse

What Do I Believe Are Signs Of Domestic Abuse?

Signs Of Domestic Abuse I Missed....

Opening Up

Opening Up

Who Is/Was Abusing Me?

Is This Type Of Abuse Normal To Me?

How Long Have I Been Abused?

The First Time I Was Abused (Write Down When):

What Kind Of Abuse Am I/Was I Experiencing?

Opening Up

My Abuser:

What Events Led Up To An Abusive Occurrence?

I Never Expected:

I Feel/Felt Like The Abuse Was My Fault Because (Answer If Applicable):

What Excuses Am I/Was I Making For My Abuser (Answer If Applicable)?

Opening Up

When I See/Saw My Abuser, I See/Saw:

When I See/Saw My Abuser, I Feel/Felt:

Other People Believe My Abuser:

The Person/People I Did Tell About What's Been Happening To Me, Have Advised Me To:

A Feeling That Will Not Go Away:

Opening Up

Because Of The Abuse, I Am No Longer Able To:

Because Of The Abuse, I Now View The World:

Because Of The Abuse, I Now View The Opposite Sex (Answer If Applicable):

Because Of The Abuse, I Now View Those Of The Same Sex (Answer If Applicable):

Abuse Has Affected My Relationships (Write In What Way):

Opening Up

Abuse Has Affected Me (Write In What Way):

I Always Feel Like I Must Accept:

Am I The First Person In My Family To Experience Abuse?

If The Answer Is No To The Previous Prompt, Who In My Family Has Experienced Abuse And How Will I Break The Pattern?

How Would I Feel Knowing My Son And/Or Daughter Was To Be Abused?

Opening Up

How Has My Family Dealt With Abuse In The Past (Answer If Applicable)?

If Someone Close To Me Does Not/Did Not Believe Me, Who Can I/Could I Turn To That I Know That Has Supported Me?

Because Of Abuse, I Deal With Conflict:

What Can I Not Control?

What Can I Control?

Opening Up

Have I 'Normalized' My Abuser's Behavior?

Why Have I Accepted Abuse For This Long (Answer If Applicable)?

What Did It Feel Like To Keep A Secret And Put On A Show For Individuals To Not Know What Was Really Going On (Answer If Applicable)?

How Do I/Did I Try To Appease My Abuser (Answer If Applicable)?

Do I Believe I Have Been Manipulated?

Opening Up

If The Answer To The Previous Prompt Is Yes, Then In What Ways Have I Been Manipulated?

I Was Manipulated To Believe That I Deserved (Answer If Applicable):

How Have I Learned To Cope With The Abuse?

Do I Believe I Can Live Without My Abuser?

What Gets Me Through The Day?

Opening Up

I Am Secretly/Publicly Getting Help For/With (Answer If Applicable):

Do I Forgive My Abuser?

Has My Abuser Threatened Me?

If Yes To The Previous Prompt, In What Way?

Has Anyone Close To My Abuser Threatened Me?

Opening Up

If Yes To The Previous Prompt, In What Way?

I Feel Like I Have Lost:

I Cannot Seem To 'Get Over':

I Feel Like I Have Changed:

Will I Ever Tell Anyone What Happened To Me?

Opening Up

Have I Seen Anyone Close To Me Be Abused?

How Long Have I Been In A Toxic Abusive Relationship (Answer If Applicable)?

I Have Stayed In A Toxic Abusive Relationship Because (Answer If Applicable)?

Do I Believe My Abuser Is Going To Change?

Based On My Response To My Previous Prompt, Why Or Why Not?

Opening Up

Will My Abuser Get Help?

Has My Abuser Ever Experienced Abuse?

I Am Scared To Lose:

I Have Seen:

I Know I Cannot Control:

Opening Up

Being Abused Has Impacted Me By:

People Around Me Tell Me:

People Around Me See:

People Around Me Say I Have:

What I Would Like To Change About My Life:

Opening Up

What I Would Like About My Life To Stay The Same:

I Believe I Deserve:

It Hurts Me When:

What Am I Willing To Change Right Now?

Do I Have A Safety Plan For Myself And My Family?

Opening Up

How Will I Stand Up For Myself?

When Will I Stand Up For Myself?

When Will I Stand Up For My Family (Answer If Applicable)?

How Will I Stand Up For My Family (Answer If Applicable)?

I Am Worthy Of:

Opening Up

I Started Realizing:

What Is Important To Me?

What Does It Mean To Live My Best Life?

Is/Was Dealing With The Abuse Worth It?

Does/Was Dealing With The Abuse Mean I Am/Was Living My Best Life?

Opening Up

I Am Tired Of:

I Can No Longer Take:

My Support System:

Who Depends On Me?

I Have Been Made To Feel:

Opening Up

I Have Been Made To Believe:

What Must Change?

What Will Change?

I Will Change For:

I Believe God:

Opening Up

It Took Time For Me To Realize:

I Am Working Through:

What Have I Survived?

What Have I Accepted In The Past That I Will No Longer Accept Now?

I Believe My Purpose In Life Is:

Opening Up

I Know There Is So Much More For Me:

I Know It Is Not Too Late To:

A Mindset I Must Break Away From:

A Loving Mindset Towards Myself:

Do I Feel Sorry For My Abuser?

Opening Up

Does Feeling Sorry For My Abuser Keep Me From Leaving (Answer If Applicable)?

I Am Breaking Free From:

I Am Forgiving Myself For:

How Would I Like To Move Forward?

Thoughts That I Have Had That Have Scared Me:

Opening Up

I Have Never Shared:

I Am Taking My Time:

A Bold Action I Am Taking For Myself:

How Will I Gain Peace?

I Am Passionate About:

Opening Up

I Am Victorious In:

I Use To Think:

I No Longer Think:

How Can I Feel Safe?

What Does My Future Look Like?

Opening Up

I Am Happy About:

What Around Me Represents Healing?

What Around Me Represents Pain?

The Lies I Have Told Myself:

How Do I Handle Conflict?

Opening Up

When Someone Yells At Me, I Feel:

How Comfortable Am I/Was I With Telling My Abuser No To Anything?

How Comfortable Am I With Saying No To Anyone About Anything?

Do I Matter?

How Do I Matter?

Opening Up

I Am Not Alone In:

My History With My Abuser:

Leaving Safely

My Leaving Safely Plan Is/Was....

When I Left

When I Left
(Answer If Applicable)....

Doing This For Me: Daily Healing

Doing This For Me: Daily Healing

Date:

I Am Worthy Of:

From Now On I Am:

No More Excuses For/Towards:

Everyday I Am Getting Better At:

Today I Am Asking God For:

I Feel:

Today I Will Stand Up For Myself By:

Today I Plan To:

Today I Will Invest In (Time, Money, Etc):

Today's Compliment To Myself:

I Am Thanking God In Advance For:

I Live In A Home That Is Free From Physical And Emotional Abuse.

Evening Thoughts

Today I Faced The Fear: _____.

Doing This For Me: Daily Healing

Date: I Feel:

I Am Worthy Of: Today I Will Stand Up For Myself By:

From Now On I Am: Today I Plan To:

No More Excuses For/Towards: Today I Will Invest In (Time, Money, Etc):

Everyday I Am Getting Better At: Today's Compliment To Myself:

Today I Am Asking God For: I Am Thanking God In Advance For:

Evening Thoughts

Today I Faced The Fear: _____.

Doing This For Me: Daily Healing

Date: I Feel:

I Am Worthy Of: Today I Will Stand Up For Myself By:

From Now On I Am: Today I Plan To:

No More Excuses For/Towards: Today I Will Invest In (Time, Money, Etc):

Everyday I Am Getting Better At: Today's Compliment To Myself:

Today I Am Asking God For: I Am Thanking God In Advance For:

Evening Thoughts

Today I Faced The Fear: _____.

I Am An Empowered Human Being. I Am Not Powerless.

It Does Get Better From Here.

I Am So Much More Than What They Think I Am.

Doing This For Me: Daily Healing

Date: I Feel:

I Am Worthy Of: Today I Will Stand Up For Myself By:

From Now On I Am: Today I Plan To:

No More Excuses For/Towards: Today I Will Invest In (Time, Money, Etc):

Everyday I Am Getting Better At: Today's Compliment To Myself:

Today I Am Asking God For: I Am Thanking God In Advance For:

Evening Thoughts

Today I Faced The Fear: _____.

Doing This For Me: Daily Healing

Date: I Feel:

I Am Worthy Of: Today I Will Stand Up For Myself By:

From Now On I Am: Today I Plan To:

No More Excuses For/Towards: Today I Will Invest In (Time, Money, Etc):

Everyday I Am Getting Better At: Today's Compliment To Myself:

Today I Am Asking God For: I Am Thanking God In Advance For:

Evening Thoughts

Today I Faced The Fear: _____.

I Am Learning That I Am Strong. I Am Learning That I Can Do What Is Right For Me.

Doing This For Me: Daily Healing

Date:

I Feel:

I Am Worthy Of:

Today I Will Stand Up For Myself By:

From Now On I Am:

Today I Plan To:

No More Excuses For/Towards:

Today I Will Invest In (Time, Money, Etc):

Everyday I Am Getting Better At:

Today's Compliment To Myself:

Today I Am Asking God For:

I Am Thanking God In Advance For:

Evening Thoughts

Today I Faced The Fear: _____.

My Thoughts

Five Motivational Songs That Keep Me Going....

1.

2.

3.

4.

5.

Doing This For Me: Daily Healing

Date:

I Am Worthy Of:

From Now On I Am:

No More Excuses For/Towards:

Everyday I Am Getting Better At:

Today I Am Asking God For:

I Feel:

Today I Will Stand Up For Myself By:

Today I Plan To:

Today I Will Invest In (Time, Money, Etc):

Today's Compliment To Myself:

I Am Thanking God In Advance For:

I Will Now Distance Myself From Anyone Who Displays Abusive Behavior.

Evening Thoughts

Today I Faced The Fear: _____.

Doing This For Me: Daily Healing

Date:

I Am Worthy Of:

From Now On I Am:

No More Excuses For/Towards:

Everyday I Am Getting Better At:

Today I Am Asking God For:

I Feel:

Today I Will Stand Up For Myself By:

Today I Plan To:

Today I Will Invest In (Time, Money, Etc):

Today's Compliment To Myself:

I Am Thanking God In Advance For:

Evening Thoughts

Today I Faced The Fear: _____.

Doing This For Me: Daily Healing

Date: I Feel:

I Am Worthy Of: Today I Will Stand Up For Myself By:

From Now On I Am: Today I Plan To:

No More Excuses For/Towards: Today I Will Invest In (Time, Money, Etc):

Everyday I Am Getting Better At: Today's Compliment To Myself:

Today I Am Asking God For: I Am Thanking God In Advance For:

There Is Nothing Wrong With Me For Choosing To Leave.

Evening Thoughts

Today I Faced The Fear: _____.

I Have Got To Be There For Me.

Greater Is He That Is In You, Than He That Is In The World.

-1 John 4:4

Doing This For Me: Daily Healing

Date:

I Am Worthy Of:

From Now On I Am:

No More Excuses For/Towards:

Everyday I Am Getting Better At:

Today I Am Asking God For:

I Feel:

Today I Will Stand Up For Myself By:

Today I Plan To:

Today I Will Invest In (Time, Money, Etc):

Today's Compliment To Myself:

I Am Thanking God In Advance For:

I Will Not Allow Other People To Mistreat Me Again.

Evening Thoughts

Today I Faced The Fear: _____.

Doing This For Me: Daily Healing

Date:

I Feel:

I Am Worthy Of:

Today I Will Stand Up For Myself By:

From Now On I Am:

Today I Plan To:

No More Excuses For/Towards:

Today I Will Invest In (Time, Money, Etc):

Everyday I Am Getting Better At:

Today's Compliment To Myself:

Today I Am Asking God For:

I Am Thanking God In Advance For:

It Is Never Alright For Anyone To Abuse Me Or Anyone Else.

Evening Thoughts

Today I Faced The Fear: _____.

Doing This For Me: Daily Healing

Date: I Feel:

I Am Worthy Of: Today I Will Stand Up For Myself By:

From Now On I Am: Today I Plan To:

No More Excuses For/Towards: Today I Will Invest In (Time, Money, Etc):

Everyday I Am Getting Better At: Today's Compliment To Myself:

Today I Am Asking God For: I Am Thanking God In Advance For:

Evening Thoughts

Today I Faced The Fear: _____.

Doing This For Me: Daily Healing

Date:

I Am Worthy Of:

From Now On I Am:

No More Excuses For/Towards:

Everyday I Am Getting Better At:

Today I Am Asking God For:

I Feel:

Today I Will Stand Up For Myself By:

Today I Plan To:

Today I Will Invest In (Time, Money, Etc):

Today's Compliment To Myself:

I Am Thanking God In Advance For:

Evening Thoughts

Today I Faced The Fear: _____.

I Know It Is Scary But I Am Starting To Make Positive Changes Right Now.

By Leaving, I Know I Would Be Saying....

By Leaving, I Know I Would Be Saying....

My Thoughts

Doing This For Me: Daily Healing

Date:

I Feel:

I Am Worthy Of:

Today I Will Stand Up For Myself By:

From Now On I Am:

Today I Plan To:

No More Excuses For/Towards:

Today I Will Invest In (Time, Money, Etc):

Everyday I Am Getting Better At:

Today's Compliment To Myself:

Today I Am Asking God For:

I Am Thanking God In Advance For:

Evening Thoughts

Today I Faced The Fear: _____.

Doing This For Me: Daily Healing

Date:

I Feel:

I Am Worthy Of:

Today I Will Stand Up For Myself By:

From Now On I Am:

Today I Plan To:

No More Excuses For/Towards:

Today I Will Invest In (Time, Money, Etc):

Everyday I Am Getting Better At:

Today's Compliment To Myself:

Today I Am Asking God For:

I Am Thanking God In Advance For:

Evening Thoughts

Today I Faced The Fear: _____.

I Am Not Falling For My Abuser's Excuses Anymore.

Doing This For Me: Daily Healing

Date:

I Am Worthy Of:

From Now On I Am:

No More Excuses For/Towards:

Everyday I Am Getting Better At:

Today I Am Asking God For:

I Feel:

Today I Will Stand Up For Myself By:

Today I Plan To:

Today I Will Invest In (Time, Money, Etc):

Today's Compliment To Myself:

I Am Thanking God In Advance For:

Evening Thoughts

Today I Faced The Fear: _____.

I Am Fully Responsible For My Own Safety.

Leaving Was The Right Choice.

Doing This For Me: Daily Healing

Date: | I Feel:

I Am Worthy Of: | Today I Will Stand Up For Myself By:

From Now On I Am: | Today I Plan To:

No More Excuses For/Towards: | Today I Will Invest In (Time, Money, Etc):

Everyday I Am Getting Better At: | Today's Compliment To Myself:

Today I Am Asking God For: | I Am Thanking God In Advance For:

Evening Thoughts

Today I Faced The Fear: _____.

I Am/Was Not To Blame For The Domestic Abuse That I Am/Was Experiencing.

Doing This For Me: Daily Healing

Date:

I Am Worthy Of:

From Now On I Am:

No More Excuses For/Towards:

Everyday I Am Getting Better At:

Today I Am Asking God For:

I Feel:

Today I Will Stand Up For Myself By:

Today I Plan To:

Today I Will Invest In (Time, Money, Etc):

Today's Compliment To Myself:

I Am Thanking God In Advance For:

I Will Not Try To Please Everybody. No One Can Do That.

Evening Thoughts

Today I Faced The Fear: _____.

Doing This For Me: Daily Healing

Date: I Feel:

I Am Worthy Of: Today I Will Stand Up For Myself By:

From Now On I Am: Today I Plan To:

No More Excuses For/Towards: Today I Will Invest In (Time, Money, Etc):

Everyday I Am Getting Better At: Today's Compliment To Myself:

Today I Am Asking God For: I Am Thanking God In Advance For:

Evening Thoughts

Today I Faced The Fear: _____.

God Placed A High Value On Me. I Am Not For Everybody.

I Deserve Better.

Doing This For Me: Daily Healing

Date: I Feel:

I Am Worthy Of: Today I Will Stand Up For Myself By:

From Now On I Am: Today I Plan To:

No More Excuses For/Towards: Today I Will Invest In (Time, Money, Etc):

Everyday I Am Getting Better At: Today's Compliment To Myself:

Today I Am Asking God For: I Am Thanking God In Advance For:

Evening Thoughts

Today I Faced The Fear: _____.

Every Decision I Make For The Betterment Of My Future Helps To Build My Self-Confidence.

Doing This For Me: Daily Healing

Date:

I Feel:

I Am Worthy Of:

Today I Will Stand Up For Myself By:

From Now On I Am:

Today I Plan To:

No More Excuses For/Towards:

Today I Will Invest In (Time, Money, Etc):

Everyday I Am Getting Better At:

Today's Compliment To Myself:

Today I Am Asking God For:

I Am Thanking God In Advance For:

My Actions Will Beget Respect From People Around Me.

Evening Thoughts

Today I Faced The Fear: _____.

Doing This For Me: Daily Healing

Date:

I Feel:

I Am Worthy Of:

Today I Will Stand Up For Myself By:

From Now On I Am:

Today I Plan To:

No More Excuses For/Towards:

Today I Will Invest In (Time, Money, Etc):

Everyday I Am Getting Better At:

Today's Compliment To Myself:

Today I Am Asking God For:

I Am Thanking God In Advance For:

Evening Thoughts

Today I Faced The Fear: _____.

I Am Making My Self-Care A Priority.

I Do Not Want To Be Judged For....

My Thoughts

Doing This For Me: Daily Healing

Date: I Feel:

I Am Worthy Of: Today I Will Stand Up For Myself By:

From Now On I Am: Today I Plan To:

No More Excuses For/Towards: Today I Will Invest In (Time, Money, Etc):

Everyday I Am Getting Better At: Today's Compliment To Myself:

Today I Am Asking God For: I Am Thanking God In Advance For:

Evening Thoughts

Today I Faced The Fear: _____.

I Am Optimistic About The Future. I Look Forward To A Better Life.

Doing This For Me: Daily Healing

Date: I Feel:

I Am Worthy Of: Today I Will Stand Up For Myself By:

From Now On I Am: Today I Plan To:

No More Excuses For/Towards: Today I Will Invest In (Time, Money, Etc):

Everyday I Am Getting Better At: Today's Compliment To Myself:

Today I Am Asking God For: I Am Thanking God In Advance For:

Evening Thoughts

Today I Faced The Fear: _____.

Doing This For Me: Daily Healing

Date:

I Am Worthy Of:

From Now On I Am:

No More Excuses For/Towards:

Everyday I Am Getting Better At:

Today I Am Asking God For:

I Feel:

Today I Will Stand Up For Myself By:

Today I Plan To:

Today I Will Invest In (Time, Money, Etc):

Today's Compliment To Myself:

I Am Thanking God In Advance For:

Evening Thoughts

Today I Faced The Fear: _____.

It Is Okay For Me To Learn About Me All Over Again.

Doing This For Me: Daily Healing

Date: I Feel:

I Am Worthy Of: Today I Will Stand Up For Myself By:

From Now On I Am: Today I Plan To:

No More Excuses For/Towards: Today I Will Invest In (Time, Money, Etc):

Everyday I Am Getting Better At: Today's Compliment To Myself:

Today I Am Asking God For: I Am Thanking God In Advance For:

Evening Thoughts

Today I Faced The Fear: _____.

I Will Not Allow Anyone To Trample On My Personal Rights.

I Am Meant To Do Great Things.

Doing This For Me: Daily Healing

Date: I Feel:

I Am Worthy Of: Today I Will Stand Up For Myself By:

From Now On I Am: Today I Plan To:

No More Excuses For/Towards: Today I Will Invest In (Time, Money, Etc):

Everyday I Am Getting Better At: Today's Compliment To Myself:

Today I Am Asking God For: I Am Thanking God In Advance For:

Evening Thoughts

Today I Faced The Fear: _____.

Doing This For Me: Daily Healing

Date:

I Am Worthy Of:

From Now On I Am:

No More Excuses For/Towards:

Everyday I Am Getting Better At:

Today I Am Asking God For:

I Feel:

Today I Will Stand Up For Myself By:

Today I Plan To:

Today I Will Invest In (Time, Money, Etc):

Today's Compliment To Myself:

I Am Thanking God In Advance For:

I Am Starting To Take Very Good Care Of Myself.

Evening Thoughts

Today I Faced The Fear: _____.

I Am No Longer Trying To Work Out....

I Am A Survivor With A Testimony.

Doing This For Me: Daily Healing

Date:

I Feel:

I Am Worthy Of:

Today I Will Stand Up For Myself By:

From Now On I Am:

Today I Plan To:

No More Excuses For/Towards:

Today I Will Invest In (Time, Money, Etc):

Everyday I Am Getting Better At:

Today's Compliment To Myself:

Today I Am Asking God For:

I Am Thanking God In Advance For:

Evening Thoughts

Today I Faced The Fear: _____.

I Will Stick With The Personal Boundaries I Put In Place For Myself.

Doing This For Me: Daily Healing

Date:

I Feel:

I Am Worthy Of:

Today I Will Stand Up For Myself By:

From Now On I Am:

Today I Plan To:

No More Excuses For/Towards:

Today I Will Invest In (Time, Money, Etc):

Everyday I Am Getting Better At:

Today's Compliment To Myself:

Today I Am Asking God For:

I Am Thanking God In Advance For:

I Enjoy The Love, Support, And Respect Of My Family.

Evening Thoughts

Today I Faced The Fear: _____.

Love Feels Good And Is Consistent.

Nothing That Happened That Resulted In Any Form Of Abuse Is My Fault.

Doing This For Me: Daily Healing

Date: I Feel:

I Am Worthy Of: Today I Will Stand Up For Myself By:

From Now On I Am: Today I Plan To:

No More Excuses For/Towards: Today I Will Invest In (Time, Money, Etc):

Everyday I Am Getting Better At: Today's Compliment To Myself:

Today I Am Asking God For: I Am Thanking God In Advance For:

Evening Thoughts

Today I Faced The Fear: _____.

Doing This For Me: Daily Healing

Date:

I Feel:

I Am Worthy Of:

Today I Will Stand Up For Myself By:

From Now On I Am:

Today I Plan To:

No More Excuses For/Towards:

Today I Will Invest In (Time, Money, Etc):

Everyday I Am Getting Better At:

Today's Compliment To Myself:

Today I Am Asking God For:

I Am Thanking God In Advance For:

Evening Thoughts

Today I Faced The Fear: _____.

My Story Will Have A Happy Ending.

Doing This For Me: Daily Healing

Date: I Feel:

I Am Worthy Of: Today I Will Stand Up For Myself By:

From Now On I Am: Today I Plan To:

No More Excuses For/Towards: Today I Will Invest In (Time, Money, Etc):

Everyday I Am Getting Better At: Today's Compliment To Myself:

Today I Am Asking God For: I Am Thanking God In Advance For:

Evening Thoughts

Today I Faced The Fear: _____.

My Thoughts

Five Things I Am Believing God For....

1.

2.

3.

4.

5.

Doing This For Me: Daily Healing

Date:

I Am Worthy Of:

From Now On I Am:

No More Excuses For/Towards:

Everyday I Am Getting Better At:

Today I Am Asking God For:

I Feel:

Today I Will Stand Up For Myself By:

Today I Plan To:

Today I Will Invest In (Time, Money, Etc):

Today's Compliment To Myself:

I Am Thanking God In Advance For:

I Have A Brand New Life To Live.

Evening Thoughts

Today I Faced The Fear: _____.

Doing This For Me: Daily Healing

Date: I Feel:

I Am Worthy Of: Today I Will Stand Up For Myself By:

From Now On I Am: Today I Plan To:

No More Excuses For/Towards: Today I Will Invest In (Time, Money, Etc):

Everyday I Am Getting Better At: Today's Compliment To Myself:

Today I Am Asking God For: I Am Thanking God In Advance For:

Evening Thoughts

Today I Faced The Fear: _____.

Doing This For Me: Daily Healing

Date:

I Am Worthy Of:

From Now On I Am:

No More Excuses For/Towards:

Everyday I Am Getting Better At:

Today I Am Asking God For:

I Feel:

Today I Will Stand Up For Myself By:

Today I Plan To:

Today I Will Invest In (Time, Money, Etc):

Today's Compliment To Myself:

I Am Thanking God In Advance For:

Evening Thoughts

Today I Faced The Fear: _____.

> Regardless Of What Happened In The Past, I Approve Of The New Life I Am Choosing For Myself That Feels Like Peace.

I Am Doing This For Me.

I Refuse To Be A Prisoner Of Someone Else's Problem.

Doing This For Me: Daily Healing

Date:

I Feel:

I Am Worthy Of:

Today I Will Stand Up For Myself By:

From Now On I Am:

Today I Plan To:

No More Excuses For/Towards:

Today I Will Invest In (Time, Money, Etc):

Everyday I Am Getting Better At:

Today's Compliment To Myself:

Today I Am Asking God For:

I Am Thanking God In Advance For:

Evening Thoughts

Today I Faced The Fear: _____.

Doing This For Me: Daily Healing

Date:

I Feel:

I Am Worthy Of:

Today I Will Stand Up For Myself By:

From Now On I Am:

Today I Plan To:

No More Excuses For/Towards:

Today I Will Invest In (Time, Money, Etc):

Everyday I Am Getting Better At:

Today's Compliment To Myself:

Today I Am Asking God For:

I Am Thanking God In Advance For:

Evening Thoughts

Today I Faced The Fear: _____.

Respect Commands Respect. That Is My Mantra.

Doing This For Me: Daily Healing

Date:

I Feel:

I Am Worthy Of:

Today I Will Stand Up For Myself By:

From Now On I Am:

Today I Plan To:

No More Excuses For/Towards:

Today I Will Invest In (Time, Money, Etc):

Everyday I Am Getting Better At:

Today's Compliment To Myself:

Today I Am Asking God For:

I Am Thanking God In Advance For:

Evening Thoughts

Today I Faced The Fear: _____.

Doing This For Me: Daily Healing

Date: I Feel:

I Am Worthy Of: Today I Will Stand Up For Myself By:

From Now On I Am: Today I Plan To:

No More Excuses For/Towards: Today I Will Invest In (Time, Money, Etc):

Everyday I Am Getting Better At: Today's Compliment To Myself:

Today I Am Asking God For: I Am Thanking God In Advance For:

Evening Thoughts

Today I Faced The Fear: _____.

My Story Is About To Turn Around And Be Filled With Bigger Miracles.

My Thoughts

Doing This For Me: Daily Healing

Date:

I Am Worthy Of:

From Now On I Am:

No More Excuses For/Towards:

Everyday I Am Getting Better At:

Today I Am Asking God For:

I Feel:

Today I Will Stand Up For Myself By:

Today I Plan To:

Today I Will Invest In (Time, Money, Etc):

Today's Compliment To Myself:

I Am Thanking God In Advance For:

Evening Thoughts

Today I Faced The Fear: _____.

> I Am Learning To Create An Environment Filled With Peace And Love. Nothing Toxic Can Ever Come In It Or From It.

Doing This For Me: Daily Healing

Date: I Feel:

I Am Worthy Of: Today I Will Stand Up For Myself By:

From Now On I Am: Today I Plan To:

No More Excuses For/Towards: Today I Will Invest In (Time, Money, Etc):

Everyday I Am Getting Better At: Today's Compliment To Myself:

Today I Am Asking God For: I Am Thanking God In Advance For:

Evening Thoughts

Today I Faced The Fear: _____.

My Well-Being Is Now My Priority. This Is My Promise To Myself.

Doing This For Me: Daily Healing

Date:

I Feel:

I Am Worthy Of:

Today I Will Stand Up For Myself By:

From Now On I Am:

Today I Plan To:

No More Excuses For/Towards:

Today I Will Invest In (Time, Money, Etc):

Everyday I Am Getting Better At:

Today's Compliment To Myself:

Today I Am Asking God For:

I Am Thanking God In Advance For:

Evening Thoughts

Today I Faced The Fear: _____.

> Things Are First Changing Inside Of Me. Next Things Will Change Around Me.

Doing This For Me: Daily Healing

Date:

I Feel:

I Am Worthy Of:

Today I Will Stand Up For Myself By:

From Now On I Am:

Today I Plan To:

No More Excuses For/Towards:

Today I Will Invest In (Time, Money, Etc):

Everyday I Am Getting Better At:

Today's Compliment To Myself:

Today I Am Asking God For:

I Am Thanking God In Advance For:

Evening Thoughts

Today I Faced The Fear: _____.

I Have Outgrown The Empty Promises.

Abuse Of Any Kind Is Not Love.

I Know I Am Capable Of....

Doing This For Me: Daily Healing

Date:

I Feel:

I Am Worthy Of:

Today I Will Stand Up For Myself By:

From Now On I Am:

Today I Plan To:

No More Excuses For/Towards:

Today I Will Invest In (Time, Money, Etc):

Everyday I Am Getting Better At:

Today's Compliment To Myself:

Today I Am Asking God For:

I Am Thanking God In Advance For:

Everyday I Am Standing Taller In My Power.

Evening Thoughts

Today I Faced The Fear: _____.

Doing This For Me: Daily Healing

Date:

I Am Worthy Of:

From Now On I Am:

No More Excuses For/Towards:

Everyday I Am Getting Better At:

Today I Am Asking God For:

I Feel:

Today I Will Stand Up For Myself By:

Today I Plan To:

Today I Will Invest In (Time, Money, Etc):

Today's Compliment To Myself:

I Am Thanking God In Advance For:

Evening Thoughts

Today I Faced The Fear: _____.

Doing This For Me: Daily Healing

Date:

I Am Worthy Of:

From Now On I Am:

No More Excuses For/Towards:

Everyday I Am Getting Better At:

Today I Am Asking God For:

I Feel:

Today I Will Stand Up For Myself By:

Today I Plan To:

Today I Will Invest In (Time, Money, Etc):

Today's Compliment To Myself:

I Am Thanking God In Advance For:

Evening Thoughts

Today I Faced The Fear: _____.

No More Excuses For Them Or For Me. I Am Taking My First Steps Towards Healing.

I Am Stronger Now.

I Am Giving Myself Permission To Leave Anything And Anyone Toxic Within My Life.

Doing This For Me: Daily Healing

Date: I Feel:

I Am Worthy Of: Today I Will Stand Up For Myself By:

From Now On I Am: Today I Plan To:

No More Excuses For/Towards: Today I Will Invest In (Time, Money, Etc):

Everyday I Am Getting Better At: Today's Compliment To Myself:

Today I Am Asking God For: I Am Thanking God In Advance For:

Evening Thoughts

Today I Faced The Fear: _____.

I Love That I Am Now Able To Sleep At Night Feeling Safe.

Doing This For Me: Daily Healing

Date:

I Am Worthy Of:

From Now On I Am:

No More Excuses For/Towards:

Everyday I Am Getting Better At:

Today I Am Asking God For:

I Feel:

Today I Will Stand Up For Myself By:

Today I Plan To:

Today I Will Invest In (Time, Money, Etc):

Today's Compliment To Myself:

I Am Thanking God In Advance For:

No More Worrying About Them. It Is Time To Focus On Me.

Evening Thoughts

Today I Faced The Fear: _____.

Doing This For Me: Daily Healing

Date:

I Feel:

I Am Worthy Of:

Today I Will Stand Up For Myself By:

From Now On I Am:

Today I Plan To:

No More Excuses For/Towards:

Today I Will Invest In (Time, Money, Etc):

Everyday I Am Getting Better At:

Today's Compliment To Myself:

Today I Am Asking God For:

I Am Thanking God In Advance For:

Evening Thoughts

Today I Faced The Fear: _____.

Doing This For Me: Daily Healing

Date:

I Am Worthy Of:

From Now On I Am:

No More Excuses For/Towards:

Everyday I Am Getting Better At:

Today I Am Asking God For:

I Feel:

Today I Will Stand Up For Myself By:

Today I Plan To:

Today I Will Invest In (Time, Money, Etc):

Today's Compliment To Myself:

I Am Thanking God In Advance For:

I Am Beautiful.

Evening Thoughts

Today I Faced The Fear: _____.

I Now Promise Myself The Best.

I Will No Longer Allow Anyone To Ever Hurt Me Again.

Doing This For Me: Daily Healing

Date: I Feel:

I Am Worthy Of: Today I Will Stand Up For Myself By:

From Now On I Am: Today I Plan To:

No More Excuses For/Towards: Today I Will Invest In (Time, Money, Etc):

Everyday I Am Getting Better At: Today's Compliment To Myself:

Today I Am Asking God For: I Am Thanking God In Advance For:

Evening Thoughts

Today I Faced The Fear: _____.

Doing This For Me: Daily Healing

Date:

I Feel:

I Am Worthy Of:

Today I Will Stand Up For Myself By:

From Now On I Am:

Today I Plan To:

No More Excuses For/Towards:

Today I Will Invest In (Time, Money, Etc):

Everyday I Am Getting Better At:

Today's Compliment To Myself:

Today I Am Asking God For:

I Am Thanking God In Advance For:

Evening Thoughts

Today I Faced The Fear: _____.

I Am My Own Responsibility.

Doing This For Me: Daily Healing

Date:

I Feel:

I Am Worthy Of:

Today I Will Stand Up For Myself By:

From Now On I Am:

Today I Plan To:

No More Excuses For/Towards:

Today I Will Invest In (Time, Money, Etc):

Everyday I Am Getting Better At:

Today's Compliment To Myself:

Today I Am Asking God For:

I Am Thanking God In Advance For:

Evening Thoughts

Today I Faced The Fear: _____.

My Thoughts

Things That Make Me Laugh....

Doing This For Me: Daily Healing

Date:

I Am Worthy Of:

From Now On I Am:

No More Excuses For/Towards:

Everyday I Am Getting Better At:

Today I Am Asking God For:

I Feel:

Today I Will Stand Up For Myself By:

Today I Plan To:

Today I Will Invest In (Time, Money, Etc):

Today's Compliment To Myself:

I Am Thanking God In Advance For:

Evening Thoughts

Today I Faced The Fear: _____.

Everything About Me Is More Than Good Enough.

Doing This For Me: Daily Healing

Date:

I Am Worthy Of:

From Now On I Am:

No More Excuses For/Towards:

Everyday I Am Getting Better At:

Today I Am Asking God For:

I Feel:

Today I Will Stand Up For Myself By:

Today I Plan To:

Today I Will Invest In (Time, Money, Etc):

Today's Compliment To Myself:

I Am Thanking God In Advance For:

Evening Thoughts

Today I Faced The Fear: _____.

I Believe That God Got Me.

Doing This For Me: Daily Healing

Date:

I Feel:

I Am Worthy Of:

Today I Will Stand Up For Myself By:

From Now On I Am:

Today I Plan To:

No More Excuses For/Towards:

Today I Will Invest In (Time, Money, Etc):

Everyday I Am Getting Better At:

Today's Compliment To Myself:

Today I Am Asking God For:

I Am Thanking God In Advance For:

Evening Thoughts

Today I Faced The Fear: _____.

Everyday I Am Becoming More Of What I Need.

Regardless If Anyone Believes It, The Truth Will Always Be The Truth.

By Freeing Myself I Am Freeing Others.

Doing This For Me: Daily Healing

Date:

I Feel:

I Am Worthy Of:

Today I Will Stand Up For Myself By:

From Now On I Am:

Today I Plan To:

No More Excuses For/Towards:

Today I Will Invest In (Time, Money, Etc):

Everyday I Am Getting Better At:

Today's Compliment To Myself:

Today I Am Asking God For:

I Am Thanking God In Advance For:

Evening Thoughts

Today I Faced The Fear: _____.

I Will Not Tolerate Anything Less Then Love.

Doing This For Me: Daily Healing

Date:

I Am Worthy Of:

From Now On I Am:

No More Excuses For/Towards:

Everyday I Am Getting Better At:

Today I Am Asking God For:

I Feel:

Today I Will Stand Up For Myself By:

Today I Plan To:

Today I Will Invest In (Time, Money, Etc):

Today's Compliment To Myself:

I Am Thanking God In Advance For:

What I Use To Get And What I Deserve Are Two Separate Things.

Evening Thoughts

Today I Faced The Fear: _____.

Doing This For Me: Daily Healing

Date:

I Am Worthy Of:

From Now On I Am:

No More Excuses For/Towards:

Everyday I Am Getting Better At:

Today I Am Asking God For:

I Feel:

Today I Will Stand Up For Myself By:

Today I Plan To:

Today I Will Invest In (Time, Money, Etc):

Today's Compliment To Myself:

I Am Thanking God In Advance For:

Evening Thoughts

Today I Faced The Fear: _____.

I Am At A Place Where I Can Walk Away.

Not One Incident Was My Fault.

Doing This For Me: Daily Healing

Date: I Feel:

I Am Worthy Of: Today I Will Stand Up For Myself By:

From Now On I Am: Today I Plan To:

No More Excuses For/Towards: Today I Will Invest In (Time, Money, Etc):

Everyday I Am Getting Better At: Today's Compliment To Myself:

Today I Am Asking God For: I Am Thanking God In Advance For:

Evening Thoughts

Today I Faced The Fear: _____.

I Am Greater Than The Situation I Am In.

Doing This For Me: Daily Healing

Date:

I Feel:

I Am Worthy Of:

Today I Will Stand Up For Myself By:

From Now On I Am:

Today I Plan To:

No More Excuses For/Towards:

Today I Will Invest In (Time, Money, Etc):

Everyday I Am Getting Better At:

Today's Compliment To Myself:

Today I Am Asking God For:

I Am Thanking God In Advance For:

I Am Letting Go Of What Hurts Me.

Evening Thoughts

Today I Faced The Fear: _____.

Doing This For Me: Daily Healing

Date: I Feel:

I Am Worthy Of: Today I Will Stand Up For Myself By:

From Now On I Am: Today I Plan To:

No More Excuses For/Towards: Today I Will Invest In (Time, Money, Etc):

Everyday I Am Getting Better At: Today's Compliment To Myself:

Today I Am Asking God For: I Am Thanking God In Advance For:

Evening Thoughts

Today I Faced The Fear: _____.

After God, I Must Be The First To Love Me Correctly.

My Thoughts

I Know I Am Never Too Old To....

Doing This For Me: Daily Healing

Date:

I Am Worthy Of:

From Now On I Am:

No More Excuses For/Towards:

Everyday I Am Getting Better At:

Today I Am Asking God For:

I Feel:

Today I Will Stand Up For Myself By:

Today I Plan To:

Today I Will Invest In (Time, Money, Etc):

Today's Compliment To Myself:

I Am Thanking God In Advance For:

Evening Thoughts

Today I Faced The Fear: _____.

I Am Worth Saving.

Doing This For Me: Daily Healing

Date: I Feel:

I Am Worthy Of: Today I Will Stand Up For Myself By:

From Now On I Am: Today I Plan To:

No More Excuses For/Towards: Today I Will Invest In (Time, Money, Etc):

Everyday I Am Getting Better At: Today's Compliment To Myself:

Today I Am Asking God For: I Am Thanking God In Advance For:

Evening Thoughts

Today I Faced The Fear: _____.

Doing This For Me: Daily Healing

Date:

I Feel:

I Am Worthy Of:

Today I Will Stand Up For Myself By:

From Now On I Am:

Today I Plan To:

No More Excuses For/Towards:

Today I Will Invest In (Time, Money, Etc):

Everyday I Am Getting Better At:

Today's Compliment To Myself:

Today I Am Asking God For:

I Am Thanking God In Advance For:

Evening Thoughts

Today I Faced The Fear: _____.

I Stopped Making Excuses. I Am Now Living In My Truth.

Everyday I Choose To Move In Peace.

Doing This For Me: Daily Healing

Date:

I Am Worthy Of:

From Now On I Am:

No More Excuses For/Towards:

Everyday I Am Getting Better At:

Today I Am Asking God For:

I Feel:

Today I Will Stand Up For Myself By:

Today I Plan To:

Today I Will Invest In (Time, Money, Etc):

Today's Compliment To Myself:

I Am Thanking God In Advance For:

I Am The Best Thing To Happen To The Right Person.

Evening Thoughts

Today I Faced The Fear: _____.

Doing This For Me: Daily Healing

Date: I Feel:

I Am Worthy Of: Today I Will Stand Up For Myself By:

From Now On I Am: Today I Plan To:

No More Excuses For/Towards: Today I Will Invest In (Time, Money, Etc):

Everyday I Am Getting Better At: Today's Compliment To Myself:

Today I Am Asking God For: I Am Thanking God In Advance For:

Evening Thoughts

Today I Faced The Fear: _____.

My Thoughts

Doing This For Me: Daily Healing

Date: I Feel:

I Am Worthy Of: Today I Will Stand Up For Myself By:

From Now On I Am: Today I Plan To:

No More Excuses For/Towards: Today I Will Invest In (Time, Money, Etc):

Everyday I Am Getting Better At: Today's Compliment To Myself:

Today I Am Asking God For: I Am Thanking God In Advance For:

Evening Thoughts

Today I Faced The Fear: _____.

Doing This For Me: Daily Healing

Date:

I Feel:

I Am Worthy Of:

Today I Will Stand Up For Myself By:

From Now On I Am:

Today I Plan To:

No More Excuses For/Towards:

Today I Will Invest In (Time, Money, Etc):

Everyday I Am Getting Better At:

Today's Compliment To Myself:

Today I Am Asking God For:

I Am Thanking God In Advance For:

Evening Thoughts

Today I Faced The Fear: _____.

Through It All I Choose To Treat Others With Love.

My Home Is A Place Where I Feel Safe.

Doing This For Me: Daily Healing

Date:

I Am Worthy Of:

From Now On I Am:

No More Excuses For/Towards:

Everyday I Am Getting Better At:

Today I Am Asking God For:

I Feel:

Today I Will Stand Up For Myself By:

Today I Plan To:

Today I Will Invest In (Time, Money, Etc):

Today's Compliment To Myself:

I Am Thanking God In Advance For:

Evening Thoughts

Today I Faced The Fear: _____.

Doing This For Me: Daily Healing

Date:

I Am Worthy Of:

From Now On I Am:

No More Excuses For/Towards:

Everyday I Am Getting Better At:

Today I Am Asking God For:

I Feel:

Today I Will Stand Up For Myself By:

Today I Plan To:

Today I Will Invest In (Time, Money, Etc):

Today's Compliment To Myself:

I Am Thanking God In Advance For:

I Am Willing To Support Me.

Evening Thoughts

Today I Faced The Fear: _____.

Doing This For Me: Daily Healing

Date:

I Feel:

I Am Worthy Of:

Today I Will Stand Up For Myself By:

From Now On I Am:

Today I Plan To:

No More Excuses For/Towards:

Today I Will Invest In (Time, Money, Etc):

Everyday I Am Getting Better At:

Today's Compliment To Myself:

Today I Am Asking God For:

I Am Thanking God In Advance For:

Evening Thoughts

Today I Faced The Fear: _____.

I Am Now Giving Myself What I Need.

My Thoughts

Doing This For Me: Daily Healing

Date: I Feel:

I Am Worthy Of: Today I Will Stand Up For Myself By:

From Now On I Am: Today I Plan To:

No More Excuses For/Towards: Today I Will Invest In (Time, Money, Etc):

Everyday I Am Getting Better At: Today's Compliment To Myself:

Today I Am Asking God For: I Am Thanking God In Advance For:

Evening Thoughts

Today I Faced The Fear: _____.

My Inner Power Transforms My Brokenness Into Something Whole.

Doing This For Me: Daily Healing

Date: I Feel:

I Am Worthy Of: Today I Will Stand Up For Myself By:

From Now On I Am: Today I Plan To:

No More Excuses For/Towards: Today I Will Invest In (Time, Money, Etc):

Everyday I Am Getting Better At: Today's Compliment To Myself:

Today I Am Asking God For: I Am Thanking God In Advance For:

Evening Thoughts

Today I Faced The Fear: _____.

Doing This For Me: Daily Healing

Date:

I Feel:

I Am Worthy Of:

Today I Will Stand Up For Myself By:

From Now On I Am:

Today I Plan To:

No More Excuses For/Towards:

Today I Will Invest In (Time, Money, Etc):

Everyday I Am Getting Better At:

Today's Compliment To Myself:

Today I Am Asking God For:

I Am Thanking God In Advance For:

Evening Thoughts

Today I Faced The Fear: _____.

I Will No Longer Allow Anything In This World To Break My Spirit.

I Am Blessed.

I Am A Warrior.

Doing This For Me: Daily Healing

Date:

I Feel:

I Am Worthy Of:

Today I Will Stand Up For Myself By:

From Now On I Am:

Today I Plan To:

No More Excuses For/Towards:

Today I Will Invest In (Time, Money, Etc):

Everyday I Am Getting Better At:

Today's Compliment To Myself:

Today I Am Asking God For:

I Am Thanking God In Advance For:

Evening Thoughts

Today I Faced The Fear: _____.

I Will Protect My Heart, My Spirit, My Mind And My Physical Body.

Doing This For Me: Daily Healing

Date: I Feel:

I Am Worthy Of: Today I Will Stand Up For Myself By:

From Now On I Am: Today I Plan To:

No More Excuses For/Towards: Today I Will Invest In (Time, Money, Etc):

Everyday I Am Getting Better At: Today's Compliment To Myself:

Today I Am Asking God For: I Am Thanking God In Advance For:

Everyday I Am Taking A Stand For Myself.

Evening Thoughts

Today I Faced The Fear: _____.

Doing This For Me: Daily Healing

Date: I Feel:

I Am Worthy Of: Today I Will Stand Up For Myself By:

From Now On I Am: Today I Plan To:

No More Excuses For/Towards: Today I Will Invest In (Time, Money, Etc):

Everyday I Am Getting Better At: Today's Compliment To Myself:

Today I Am Asking God For: I Am Thanking God In Advance For:

Evening Thoughts

Today I Faced The Fear: _____.

Doing This For Me: Daily Healing

Date: I Feel:

I Am Worthy Of: Today I Will Stand Up For Myself By:

From Now On I Am: Today I Plan To:

No More Excuses For/Towards: Today I Will Invest In (Time, Money, Etc):

Everyday I Am Getting Better At: Today's Compliment To Myself:

Today I Am Asking God For: I Am Thanking God In Advance For:

I Am Healing One Day And One Step At A Time.

Evening Thoughts

Today I Faced The Fear: _____.

I Am Speaking Up For Me.

I Am Amazing.

Doing This For Me: Daily Healing

Date: I Feel:

I Am Worthy Of: Today I Will Stand Up For Myself By:

From Now On I Am: Today I Plan To:

No More Excuses For/Towards: Today I Will Invest In (Time, Money, Etc):

Everyday I Am Getting Better At: Today's Compliment To Myself:

Today I Am Asking God For: I Am Thanking God In Advance For:

Evening Thoughts

Today I Faced The Fear: _____.

Doing This For Me: Daily Healing

Date:

I Am Worthy Of:

From Now On I Am:

No More Excuses For/Towards:

Everyday I Am Getting Better At:

Today I Am Asking God For:

I Feel:

Today I Will Stand Up For Myself By:

Today I Plan To:

Today I Will Invest In (Time, Money, Etc):

Today's Compliment To Myself:

I Am Thanking God In Advance For:

I Deserve Happiness. I Deserve To Live Pain Free.

Evening Thoughts

Today I Faced The Fear: _____.

Doing This For Me: Daily Healing

Date: I Feel:

I Am Worthy Of: Today I Will Stand Up For Myself By:

From Now On I Am: Today I Plan To:

No More Excuses For/Towards: Today I Will Invest In (Time, Money, Etc):

Everyday I Am Getting Better At: Today's Compliment To Myself:

Today I Am Asking God For: I Am Thanking God In Advance For:

Evening Thoughts

Today I Faced The Fear: _____.

I Forgive The People Who Have Done Me Wrong.

The Timing Is Perfect.

What Will Save My Heart?

Doing This For Me: Daily Healing

Date:

I Feel:

I Am Worthy Of:

Today I Will Stand Up For Myself By:

From Now On I Am:

Today I Plan To:

No More Excuses For/Towards:

Today I Will Invest In (Time, Money, Etc):

Everyday I Am Getting Better At:

Today's Compliment To Myself:

Today I Am Asking God For:

I Am Thanking God In Advance For:

Evening Thoughts

Today I Faced The Fear: _____.

> Anyone Coming Into My Life As A Friend Or More Must Like Me As Much As I Like Me Or More.

Doing This For Me: Daily Healing

Date:

I Feel:

I Am Worthy Of:

Today I Will Stand Up For Myself By:

From Now On I Am:

Today I Plan To:

No More Excuses For/Towards:

Today I Will Invest In (Time, Money, Etc):

Everyday I Am Getting Better At:

Today's Compliment To Myself:

Today I Am Asking God For:

I Am Thanking God In Advance For:

Evening Thoughts

Today I Faced The Fear: _____.

No Longer Will I Settle.

Doing This For Me: Daily Healing

Date:

I Feel:

I Am Worthy Of:

Today I Will Stand Up For Myself By:

From Now On I Am:

Today I Plan To:

No More Excuses For/Towards:

Today I Will Invest In (Time, Money, Etc):

Everyday I Am Getting Better At:

Today's Compliment To Myself:

Today I Am Asking God For:

I Am Thanking God In Advance For:

Evening Thoughts

Today I Faced The Fear: _____.

I Will Listen To My Spirit More.

All I Can Do Is Take It One Day At A Time.

I Am Not Damaged. I Am Lovable.

Doing This For Me: Daily Healing

Date: I Feel:

I Am Worthy Of: Today I Will Stand Up For Myself By:

From Now On I Am: Today I Plan To:

No More Excuses For/Towards: Today I Will Invest In (Time, Money, Etc):

Everyday I Am Getting Better At: Today's Compliment To Myself:

Today I Am Asking God For: I Am Thanking God In Advance For:

Evening Thoughts

Today I Faced The Fear: _____.

I Have The Right To Enjoy The Best Things That Life Has To Offer.

Doing This For Me: Daily Healing

Date: I Feel:

I Am Worthy Of: Today I Will Stand Up For Myself By:

From Now On I Am: Today I Plan To:

No More Excuses For/Towards: Today I Will Invest In (Time, Money, Etc):

Everyday I Am Getting Better At: Today's Compliment To Myself:

Today I Am Asking God For: I Am Thanking God In Advance For:

My Life Will Be Lived With Complete Honesty Towards Myself.

Evening Thoughts

Today I Faced The Fear: _____.

Doing This For Me: Daily Healing

Date:

I Feel:

I Am Worthy Of:

Today I Will Stand Up For Myself By:

From Now On I Am:

Today I Plan To:

No More Excuses For/Towards:

Today I Will Invest In (Time, Money, Etc):

Everyday I Am Getting Better At:

Today's Compliment To Myself:

Today I Am Asking God For:

I Am Thanking God In Advance For:

Evening Thoughts

Today I Faced The Fear: _____.

My Thoughts

Doing This For Me: Daily Healing

Date:

I Am Worthy Of:

From Now On I Am:

No More Excuses For/Towards:

Everyday I Am Getting Better At:

Today I Am Asking God For:

I Feel:

Today I Will Stand Up For Myself By:

Today I Plan To:

Today I Will Invest In (Time, Money, Etc):

Today's Compliment To Myself:

I Am Thanking God In Advance For:

I Am Giving Myself Love And Time To Heal.

Evening Thoughts

Today I Faced The Fear: _____.

Doing This For Me: Daily Healing

Date:

I Am Worthy Of:

From Now On I Am:

No More Excuses For/Towards:

Everyday I Am Getting Better At:

Today I Am Asking God For:

I Feel:

Today I Will Stand Up For Myself By:

Today I Plan To:

Today I Will Invest In (Time, Money, Etc):

Today's Compliment To Myself:

I Am Thanking God In Advance For:

Evening Thoughts

Today I Faced The Fear: _____.

I Know That The People Around Me Are Cheering Me On.

Doing This For Me: Daily Healing

Date:

I Feel:

I Am Worthy Of:

Today I Will Stand Up For Myself By:

From Now On I Am:

Today I Plan To:

No More Excuses For/Towards:

Today I Will Invest In (Time, Money, Etc):

Everyday I Am Getting Better At:

Today's Compliment To Myself:

Today I Am Asking God For:

I Am Thanking God In Advance For:

Evening Thoughts

Today I Faced The Fear: _____.

I Am Not Defined By What Happened To Me. I Am Who I Choose To Become.

Doing This For Me: Daily Healing

Date:

I Feel:

I Am Worthy Of:

Today I Will Stand Up For Myself By:

From Now On I Am:

Today I Plan To:

No More Excuses For/Towards:

Today I Will Invest In (Time, Money, Etc):

Everyday I Am Getting Better At:

Today's Compliment To Myself:

Today I Am Asking God For:

I Am Thanking God In Advance For:

Evening Thoughts

Today I Faced The Fear: _____.

Everything That I Want To Change All Starts Within Myself.

Doing This For Me: Daily Healing

Date:

I Am Worthy Of:

From Now On I Am:

No More Excuses For/Towards:

Everyday I Am Getting Better At:

Today I Am Asking God For:

I Feel:

Today I Will Stand Up For Myself By:

Today I Plan To:

Today I Will Invest In (Time, Money, Etc):

Today's Compliment To Myself:

I Am Thanking God In Advance For:

What I Once Said Yes To I Am Now Saying No To.

Evening Thoughts

Today I Faced The Fear: _____.

The Things I Want To Change....

Doing This For Me: Daily Healing

Date:

I Feel:

I Am Worthy Of:

Today I Will Stand Up For Myself By:

From Now On I Am:

Today I Plan To:

No More Excuses For/Towards:

Today I Will Invest In (Time, Money, Etc):

Everyday I Am Getting Better At:

Today's Compliment To Myself:

Today I Am Asking God For:

I Am Thanking God In Advance For:

I Will Not Let Anyone Make A Victim Out Of Me Again.

Evening Thoughts

Today I Faced The Fear: _____.

Doing This For Me: Daily Healing

Date:

I Feel:

I Am Worthy Of:

Today I Will Stand Up For Myself By:

From Now On I Am:

Today I Plan To:

No More Excuses For/Towards:

Today I Will Invest In (Time, Money, Etc):

Everyday I Am Getting Better At:

Today's Compliment To Myself:

Today I Am Asking God For:

I Am Thanking God In Advance For:

Evening Thoughts

Today I Faced The Fear: _____.

It Is My Job To Love And Respect Me And Release Everything And Everyone That Does Not.

Doing This For Me: Daily Healing

Date: I Feel:

I Am Worthy Of: Today I Will Stand Up For Myself By:

From Now On I Am: Today I Plan To:

No More Excuses For/Towards: Today I Will Invest In (Time, Money, Etc):

Everyday I Am Getting Better At: Today's Compliment To Myself:

Today I Am Asking God For: I Am Thanking God In Advance For:

Evening Thoughts

Today I Faced The Fear: _____.

I Will Not Force Other People To View Me The Way I Wish They Would.

Things Are Starting To Come Together.

The Pain I Have Experienced Will Not Cause Me To Hate.

Doing This For Me: Daily Healing

Date:

I Feel:

I Am Worthy Of:

Today I Will Stand Up For Myself By:

From Now On I Am:

Today I Plan To:

No More Excuses For/Towards:

Today I Will Invest In (Time, Money, Etc):

Everyday I Am Getting Better At:

Today's Compliment To Myself:

Today I Am Asking God For:

I Am Thanking God In Advance For:

Evening Thoughts

Today I Faced The Fear: _____.

I Will Never Be The Cause Of Any Violence.

Doing This For Me: Daily Healing

Date:

I Am Worthy Of:

From Now On I Am:

No More Excuses For/Towards:

Everyday I Am Getting Better At:

Today I Am Asking God For:

I Feel:

Today I Will Stand Up For Myself By:

Today I Plan To:

Today I Will Invest In (Time, Money, Etc):

Today's Compliment To Myself:

I Am Thanking God In Advance For:

Evening Thoughts

Today I Faced The Fear: _____.

I Am Not Afraid To Rebuild From Scratch.

Doing This For Me: Daily Healing

Date:

I Am Worthy Of:

From Now On I Am:

No More Excuses For/Towards:

Everyday I Am Getting Better At:

Today I Am Asking God For:

I Feel:

Today I Will Stand Up For Myself By:

Today I Plan To:

Today I Will Invest In (Time, Money, Etc):

Today's Compliment To Myself:

I Am Thanking God In Advance For:

Any Abuse Done To Me Does Not Degrade Me; It Degrades My Abuser.

Evening Thoughts

Today I Faced The Fear: _____.

My Thoughts

Five Years From Today, I See Myself....

Doing This For Me: Daily Healing

Date:

I Feel:

I Am Worthy Of:

Today I Will Stand Up For Myself By:

From Now On I Am:

Today I Plan To:

No More Excuses For/Towards:

Today I Will Invest In (Time, Money, Etc):

Everyday I Am Getting Better At:

Today's Compliment To Myself:

Today I Am Asking God For:

I Am Thanking God In Advance For:

Evening Thoughts

Today I Faced The Fear: _____.

I Am Learning How Amazing I Can Be.

Doing This For Me: Daily Healing

Date: I Feel:

I Am Worthy Of: Today I Will Stand Up For Myself By:

From Now On I Am: Today I Plan To:

No More Excuses For/Towards: Today I Will Invest In (Time, Money, Etc):

Everyday I Am Getting Better At: Today's Compliment To Myself:

Today I Am Asking God For: I Am Thanking God In Advance For:

Evening Thoughts

Today I Faced The Fear: _____.

Doing This For Me: Daily Healing

Date:	I Feel:

I Am Worthy Of:	Today I Will Stand Up For Myself By:

From Now On I Am:	Today I Plan To:

No More Excuses For/Towards:	Today I Will Invest In (Time, Money, Etc):

Everyday I Am Getting Better At:	Today's Compliment To Myself:

Today I Am Asking God For:	I Am Thanking God In Advance For:

Evening Thoughts

Today I Faced The Fear: _____.

No Longer Will I Entertain Negative Thoughts Towards Myself.

I Am Sorry.

- A Note To Myself

There Is Sunshine After The Rain.

Doing This For Me: Daily Healing

Date: I Feel:

I Am Worthy Of: Today I Will Stand Up For Myself By:

From Now On I Am: Today I Plan To:

No More Excuses For/Towards: Today I Will Invest In (Time, Money, Etc):

Everyday I Am Getting Better At: Today's Compliment To Myself:

Today I Am Asking God For: I Am Thanking God In Advance For:

Evening Thoughts

Today I Faced The Fear: _____.

Doing This For Me: Daily Healing

Date:

I Feel:

I Am Worthy Of:

Today I Will Stand Up For Myself By:

From Now On I Am:

Today I Plan To:

No More Excuses For/Towards:

Today I Will Invest In (Time, Money, Etc):

Everyday I Am Getting Better At:

Today's Compliment To Myself:

Today I Am Asking God For:

I Am Thanking God In Advance For:

Evening Thoughts

Today I Faced The Fear: _____.

To Be Happy, Successful, And Healthy Is My Right.

Doing This For Me: Daily Healing

Date:

I Feel:

I Am Worthy Of:

Today I Will Stand Up For Myself By:

From Now On I Am:

Today I Plan To:

No More Excuses For/Towards:

Today I Will Invest In (Time, Money, Etc):

Everyday I Am Getting Better At:

Today's Compliment To Myself:

Today I Am Asking God For:

I Am Thanking God In Advance For:

Evening Thoughts

Today I Faced The Fear: _____.

I Will Not Judge; I Will Only Help Other Victims In Their Healing.

A Year From Today, I Want To....

Seven People Who Inspire Me....

1.

2.

3.

4.

5.

6.

7.

Doing This For Me: Daily Healing

Date: I Feel:

I Am Worthy Of: Today I Will Stand Up For Myself By:

From Now On I Am: Today I Plan To:

No More Excuses For/Towards: Today I Will Invest In (Time, Money, Etc):

Everyday I Am Getting Better At: Today's Compliment To Myself:

Today I Am Asking God For: I Am Thanking God In Advance For:

I Will Be Careful With How I Speak To Myself.

Evening Thoughts

Today I Faced The Fear: _____.

Doing This For Me: Daily Healing

Date: I Feel:

I Am Worthy Of: Today I Will Stand Up For Myself By:

From Now On I Am: Today I Plan To:

No More Excuses For/Towards: Today I Will Invest In (Time, Money, Etc):

Everyday I Am Getting Better At: Today's Compliment To Myself:

Today I Am Asking God For: I Am Thanking God In Advance For:

Evening Thoughts

Today I Faced The Fear: _____.

Doing This For Me: Daily Healing

Date:

I Am Worthy Of:

From Now On I Am:

No More Excuses For/Towards:

Everyday I Am Getting Better At:

Today I Am Asking God For:

I Feel:

Today I Will Stand Up For Myself By:

Today I Plan To:

Today I Will Invest In (Time, Money, Etc):

Today's Compliment To Myself:

I Am Thanking God In Advance For:

Evening Thoughts

Today I Faced The Fear: _____.

I Do Not Need Anyone's Approval To Do What Is Best For My Well-Being.

This Is A New Me.

Now When I Say No I Mean It.

Doing This For Me: Daily Healing

Date: I Feel:

I Am Worthy Of: Today I Will Stand Up For Myself By:

From Now On I Am: Today I Plan To:

No More Excuses For/Towards: Today I Will Invest In (Time, Money, Etc):

Everyday I Am Getting Better At: Today's Compliment To Myself:

Today I Am Asking God For: I Am Thanking God In Advance For:

Evening Thoughts

Today I Faced The Fear: _____.

If Gaining Peace Of Mind Means Losing It All Then I Am Not Losing Anything.

Doing This For Me: Daily Healing

Date: I Feel:

I Am Worthy Of: Today I Will Stand Up For Myself By:

From Now On I Am: Today I Plan To:

No More Excuses For/Towards: Today I Will Invest In (Time, Money, Etc):

Everyday I Am Getting Better At: Today's Compliment To Myself:

Today I Am Asking God For: I Am Thanking God In Advance For:

Evening Thoughts

Today I Faced The Fear: _____.

I Am No Longer Alone. I Have My Family And Friends With Me.

Doing This For Me: Daily Healing

Date: I Feel:

I Am Worthy Of: Today I Will Stand Up For Myself By:

From Now On I Am: Today I Plan To:

No More Excuses For/Towards: Today I Will Invest In (Time, Money, Etc):

Everyday I Am Getting Better At: Today's Compliment To Myself:

Today I Am Asking God For: I Am Thanking God In Advance For:

Evening Thoughts

Today I Faced The Fear: _____.

Each Day I Am Working Up My Ability To Walk Away.

Doing This For Me: Daily Healing

Date:

I Am Worthy Of:

From Now On I Am:

No More Excuses For/Towards:

Everyday I Am Getting Better At:

Today I Am Asking God For:

I Feel:

Today I Will Stand Up For Myself By:

Today I Plan To:

Today I Will Invest In (Time, Money, Etc):

Today's Compliment To Myself:

I Am Thanking God In Advance For:

I Am So Much More Than What They Have Tried To Reduce Me To.

Evening Thoughts

Today I Faced The Fear: _____.

My God Provided A Way Out.

I Am Learning From My Past.

Doing This For Me: Daily Healing

Date: I Feel:

I Am Worthy Of: Today I Will Stand Up For Myself By:

From Now On I Am: Today I Plan To:

No More Excuses For/Towards: Today I Will Invest In (Time, Money, Etc):

Everyday I Am Getting Better At: Today's Compliment To Myself:

Today I Am Asking God For: I Am Thanking God In Advance For:

Evening Thoughts

Today I Faced The Fear: _____.

I Am So Much More Than What They Have Taught Me To Believe.

Doing This For Me: Daily Healing

Date: I Feel:

I Am Worthy Of: Today I Will Stand Up For Myself By:

From Now On I Am: Today I Plan To:

No More Excuses For/Towards: Today I Will Invest In (Time, Money, Etc):

Everyday I Am Getting Better At: Today's Compliment To Myself:

Today I Am Asking God For: I Am Thanking God In Advance For:

Evening Thoughts

Today I Faced The Fear: _____.

I Am Not The Reason For Someone Else's Anger.

Doing This For Me: Daily Healing

Date: I Feel:

I Am Worthy Of: Today I Will Stand Up For Myself By:

From Now On I Am: Today I Plan To:

No More Excuses For/Towards: Today I Will Invest In (Time, Money, Etc):

Everyday I Am Getting Better At: Today's Compliment To Myself:

Today I Am Asking God For: I Am Thanking God In Advance For:

Evening Thoughts

Today I Faced The Fear: _____.

I Will Not Allow Fear To Become Bigger Than The Actual Action I Need To Take.

My Thoughts

Doing This For Me: Daily Healing

Date: I Feel:

I Am Worthy Of: Today I Will Stand Up For Myself By:

From Now On I Am: Today I Plan To:

No More Excuses For/Towards: Today I Will Invest In (Time, Money, Etc):

Everyday I Am Getting Better At: Today's Compliment To Myself:

Today I Am Asking God For: I Am Thanking God In Advance For:

Evening Thoughts

Today I Faced The Fear: _____.

It Is A Brand New Day To Say Yes To Me.

Doing This For Me: Daily Healing

Date:

I Am Worthy Of:

From Now On I Am:

No More Excuses For/Towards:

Everyday I Am Getting Better At:

Today I Am Asking God For:

I Feel:

Today I Will Stand Up For Myself By:

Today I Plan To:

Today I Will Invest In (Time, Money, Etc):

Today's Compliment To Myself:

I Am Thanking God In Advance For:

I Will Never Give Anyone The Right To Abuse Me.

Evening Thoughts

Today I Faced The Fear: _____.

Doing This For Me: Daily Healing

Date:

I Feel:

I Am Worthy Of:

Today I Will Stand Up For Myself By:

From Now On I Am:

Today I Plan To:

No More Excuses For/Towards:

Today I Will Invest In (Time, Money, Etc):

Everyday I Am Getting Better At:

Today's Compliment To Myself:

Today I Am Asking God For:

I Am Thanking God In Advance For:

Evening Thoughts

Today I Faced The Fear: _____.

It Is Okay If I Stand Up For Myself By Leaving.

I Have Hope. I Have Faith.

Being Strong Was My Only Option.

Doing This For Me: Daily Healing

Date: I Feel:

I Am Worthy Of: Today I Will Stand Up For Myself By:

From Now On I Am: Today I Plan To:

No More Excuses For/Towards: Today I Will Invest In (Time, Money, Etc):

Everyday I Am Getting Better At: Today's Compliment To Myself:

Today I Am Asking God For: I Am Thanking God In Advance For:

Evening Thoughts

Today I Faced The Fear: _____.

No One In This World Deserves To Be Abused – Including Me.

Doing This For Me: Daily Healing

Date:

I Am Worthy Of:

From Now On I Am:

No More Excuses For/Towards:

Everyday I Am Getting Better At:

Today I Am Asking God For:

I Feel:

Today I Will Stand Up For Myself By:

Today I Plan To:

Today I Will Invest In (Time, Money, Etc):

Today's Compliment To Myself:

I Am Thanking God In Advance For:

Every Step I Take To Move Forward Is A Step Towards A Better Tomorrow.

Evening Thoughts

Today I Faced The Fear: _____.

Doing This For Me: Daily Healing

Date:

I Feel:

I Am Worthy Of:

Today I Will Stand Up For Myself By:

From Now On I Am:

Today I Plan To:

No More Excuses For/Towards:

Today I Will Invest In (Time, Money, Etc):

Everyday I Am Getting Better At:

Today's Compliment To Myself:

Today I Am Asking God For:

I Am Thanking God In Advance For:

Evening Thoughts

Today I Faced The Fear: _____.

I Know God Loves Me. I Know That There Is Better For Me.

Things I Have Learned Within The Past Few Months About Myself....

Doing This For Me: Daily Healing

Date:

I Feel:

I Am Worthy Of:

Today I Will Stand Up For Myself By:

From Now On I Am:

Today I Plan To:

No More Excuses For/Towards:

Today I Will Invest In (Time, Money, Etc):

Everyday I Am Getting Better At:

Today's Compliment To Myself:

Today I Am Asking God For:

I Am Thanking God In Advance For:

Evening Thoughts

Today I Faced The Fear: _____.

Doing This For Me: Daily Healing

Date: I Feel:

I Am Worthy Of: Today I Will Stand Up For Myself By:

From Now On I Am: Today I Plan To:

No More Excuses For/Towards: Today I Will Invest In (Time, Money, Etc):

Everyday I Am Getting Better At: Today's Compliment To Myself:

Today I Am Asking God For: I Am Thanking God In Advance For:

Evening Thoughts

Today I Faced The Fear: _____.

Doing This For Me: Daily Healing

Date:

I Feel:

I Am Worthy Of:

Today I Will Stand Up For Myself By:

From Now On I Am:

Today I Plan To:

No More Excuses For/Towards:

Today I Will Invest In (Time, Money, Etc):

Everyday I Am Getting Better At:

Today's Compliment To Myself:

Today I Am Asking God For:

I Am Thanking God In Advance For:

Evening Thoughts

Today I Faced The Fear: _____.

I Have So Many Wonderful Things That Are Happening For Me.

Doing This For Me: Daily Healing

Date:

I Am Worthy Of:

From Now On I Am:

No More Excuses For/Towards:

Everyday I Am Getting Better At:

Today I Am Asking God For:

I Feel:

Today I Will Stand Up For Myself By:

Today I Plan To:

Today I Will Invest In (Time, Money, Etc):

Today's Compliment To Myself:

I Am Thanking God In Advance For:

Evening Thoughts

Today I Faced The Fear: _____.

If It Threatens My Peace Of Mind, I Will Walk Away From It.

Doing This For Me: Daily Healing

Date: I Feel:

I Am Worthy Of: Today I Will Stand Up For Myself By:

From Now On I Am: Today I Plan To:

No More Excuses For/Towards: Today I Will Invest In (Time, Money, Etc):

Everyday I Am Getting Better At: Today's Compliment To Myself:

Today I Am Asking God For: I Am Thanking God In Advance For:

From Now On I Will Always Be The First Person To Protect Me.

Evening Thoughts

Today I Faced The Fear: _____.

Doing This For Me: Daily Healing

Date:

I Feel:

I Am Worthy Of:

Today I Will Stand Up For Myself By:

From Now On I Am:

Today I Plan To:

No More Excuses For/Towards:

Today I Will Invest In (Time, Money, Etc):

Everyday I Am Getting Better At:

Today's Compliment To Myself:

Today I Am Asking God For:

I Am Thanking God In Advance For:

Evening Thoughts

Today I Faced The Fear: _____.

I Am Finding Value Within Myself.

Doing This For Me: Daily Healing

Date: I Feel:

I Am Worthy Of: Today I Will Stand Up For Myself By:

From Now On I Am: Today I Plan To:

No More Excuses For/Towards: Today I Will Invest In (Time, Money, Etc):

Everyday I Am Getting Better At: Today's Compliment To Myself:

Today I Am Asking God For: I Am Thanking God In Advance For:

Evening Thoughts

Today I Faced The Fear: _____.

I Need To Live In Safety.

The Lord Is My Shepherd.

My Story Will Save Someone.

Doing This For Me: Daily Healing

Date:

I Feel:

I Am Worthy Of:

Today I Will Stand Up For Myself By:

From Now On I Am:

Today I Plan To:

No More Excuses For/Towards:

Today I Will Invest In (Time, Money, Etc):

Everyday I Am Getting Better At:

Today's Compliment To Myself:

Today I Am Asking God For:

I Am Thanking God In Advance For:

Evening Thoughts

Today I Faced The Fear: _____.

Doing This For Me: Daily Healing

Date: I Feel:

I Am Worthy Of: Today I Will Stand Up For Myself By:

From Now On I Am: Today I Plan To:

No More Excuses For/Towards: Today I Will Invest In (Time, Money, Etc):

Everyday I Am Getting Better At: Today's Compliment To Myself:

Today I Am Asking God For: I Am Thanking God In Advance For:

Evening Thoughts

Today I Faced The Fear: _____.

No Longer Will I Allow My Abuser To Control Me.

Doing This For Me: Daily Healing

Date: I Feel:

I Am Worthy Of: Today I Will Stand Up For Myself By:

From Now On I Am: Today I Plan To:

No More Excuses For/Towards: Today I Will Invest In (Time, Money, Etc):

Everyday I Am Getting Better At: Today's Compliment To Myself:

Today I Am Asking God For: I Am Thanking God In Advance For:

Evening Thoughts

Today I Faced The Fear: _____.

Everyday Is A Chance To Start Over.

Doing This For Me: Daily Healing

Date: I Feel:

I Am Worthy Of: Today I Will Stand Up For Myself By:

From Now On I Am: Today I Plan To:

No More Excuses For/Towards: Today I Will Invest In (Time, Money, Etc):

Everyday I Am Getting Better At: Today's Compliment To Myself:

Today I Am Asking God For: I Am Thanking God In Advance For:

Evening Thoughts

Today I Faced The Fear: _____.

Doing This For Me: Daily Healing

Date:

I Feel:

I Am Worthy Of:

Today I Will Stand Up For Myself By:

From Now On I Am:

Today I Plan To:

No More Excuses For/Towards:

Today I Will Invest In (Time, Money, Etc):

Everyday I Am Getting Better At:

Today's Compliment To Myself:

Today I Am Asking God For:

I Am Thanking God In Advance For:

Evening Thoughts

Today I Faced The Fear: _____.

Giving Some Of The Love I Give To Others To Myself.

Doing This For Me: Daily Healing

Date:

I Feel:

I Am Worthy Of:

Today I Will Stand Up For Myself By:

From Now On I Am:

Today I Plan To:

No More Excuses For/Towards:

Today I Will Invest In (Time, Money, Etc):

Everyday I Am Getting Better At:

Today's Compliment To Myself:

Today I Am Asking God For:

I Am Thanking God In Advance For:

Evening Thoughts

Today I Faced The Fear: _____.

I Will Not Grow Tired In Protecting Me.

Doing This For Me: Daily Healing

Date:

I Feel:

I Am Worthy Of:

Today I Will Stand Up For Myself By:

From Now On I Am:

Today I Plan To:

No More Excuses For/Towards:

Today I Will Invest In (Time, Money, Etc):

Everyday I Am Getting Better At:

Today's Compliment To Myself:

Today I Am Asking God For:

I Am Thanking God In Advance For:

Evening Thoughts

Today I Faced The Fear: _____.

I Deserve Real Love. Real Love Does Not Hurt Me.

My Thoughts

Doing This For Me: Daily Healing

Date:

I Feel:

I Am Worthy Of:

Today I Will Stand Up For Myself By:

From Now On I Am:

Today I Plan To:

No More Excuses For/Towards:

Today I Will Invest In (Time, Money, Etc):

Everyday I Am Getting Better At:

Today's Compliment To Myself:

Today I Am Asking God For:

I Am Thanking God In Advance For:

Evening Thoughts

Today I Faced The Fear: _____.

If I Cannot Be Myself Then It Is Not For Me.

Doing This For Me: Daily Healing

Date:

I Feel:

I Am Worthy Of:

Today I Will Stand Up For Myself By:

From Now On I Am:

Today I Plan To:

No More Excuses For/Towards:

Today I Will Invest In (Time, Money, Etc):

Everyday I Am Getting Better At:

Today's Compliment To Myself:

Today I Am Asking God For:

I Am Thanking God In Advance For:

Evening Thoughts

Today I Faced The Fear: _____.

A Peaceful Life Belongs To Me.

Doing This For Me: Daily Healing

Date: I Feel:

I Am Worthy Of: Today I Will Stand Up For Myself By:

From Now On I Am: Today I Plan To:

No More Excuses For/Towards: Today I Will Invest In (Time, Money, Etc):

Everyday I Am Getting Better At: Today's Compliment To Myself:

Today I Am Asking God For: I Am Thanking God In Advance For:

Evening Thoughts

Today I Faced The Fear: _____.

I Will Not Allow Fear To Hold Me Back From Freedom.

I Will Be My Own Best Friend.

Doing This For Me: Daily Healing

Date:

I Am Worthy Of:

From Now On I Am:

No More Excuses For/Towards:

Everyday I Am Getting Better At:

Today I Am Asking God For:

I Feel:

Today I Will Stand Up For Myself By:

Today I Plan To:

Today I Will Invest In (Time, Money, Etc):

Today's Compliment To Myself:

I Am Thanking God In Advance For:

I Am A Good Person Who Is Worthy Of Being Loved Correctly.

Evening Thoughts

Today I Faced The Fear: _____.

Doing This For Me: Daily Healing

Date:

I Feel:

I Am Worthy Of:

Today I Will Stand Up For Myself By:

From Now On I Am:

Today I Plan To:

No More Excuses For/Towards:

Today I Will Invest In (Time, Money, Etc):

Everyday I Am Getting Better At:

Today's Compliment To Myself:

Today I Am Asking God For:

I Am Thanking God In Advance For:

Evening Thoughts

Today I Faced The Fear: _____.

*I Am Not Ashamed.
I Am Empowered.*

Doing This For Me: Daily Healing

Date:

I Feel:

I Am Worthy Of:

Today I Will Stand Up For Myself By:

From Now On I Am:

Today I Plan To:

No More Excuses For/Towards:

Today I Will Invest In (Time, Money, Etc):

Everyday I Am Getting Better At:

Today's Compliment To Myself:

Today I Am Asking God For:

I Am Thanking God In Advance For:

Evening Thoughts

Today I Faced The Fear: _____.

I Do Not Deserve For Anyone To Punish Me.

Doing This For Me: Daily Healing

Date:

I Feel:

I Am Worthy Of:

Today I Will Stand Up For Myself By:

From Now On I Am:

Today I Plan To:

No More Excuses For/Towards:

Today I Will Invest In (Time, Money, Etc):

Everyday I Am Getting Better At:

Today's Compliment To Myself:

Today I Am Asking God For:

I Am Thanking God In Advance For:

I Will Not Survive Off Of Only Apologies And Temporary Changes.

Evening Thoughts

Today I Faced The Fear: _____.

Doing This For Me: Daily Healing

Date:

I Feel:

I Am Worthy Of:

Today I Will Stand Up For Myself By:

From Now On I Am:

Today I Plan To:

No More Excuses For/Towards:

Today I Will Invest In (Time, Money, Etc):

Everyday I Am Getting Better At:

Today's Compliment To Myself:

Today I Am Asking God For:

I Am Thanking God In Advance For:

Evening Thoughts

Today I Faced The Fear: _____.

My Change For The Better Will Start Within Me.

My Thoughts

Doing This For Me: Daily Healing

Date:

I Am Worthy Of:

From Now On I Am:

No More Excuses For/Towards:

Everyday I Am Getting Better At:

Today I Am Asking God For:

I Feel:

Today I Will Stand Up For Myself By:

Today I Plan To:

Today I Will Invest In (Time, Money, Etc):

Today's Compliment To Myself:

I Am Thanking God In Advance For:

I Can No Longer Depend On The Good Times Of The Past.

Evening Thoughts

Today I Faced The Fear: _____.

Doing This For Me: Daily Healing

Date:

I Am Worthy Of:

From Now On I Am:

No More Excuses For/Towards:

Everyday I Am Getting Better At:

Today I Am Asking God For:

I Feel:

Today I Will Stand Up For Myself By:

Today I Plan To:

Today I Will Invest In (Time, Money, Etc):

Today's Compliment To Myself:

I Am Thanking God In Advance For:

I Will Not Resist The People Who Only Want To Help Me Get Better.

Evening Thoughts

Today I Faced The Fear: _____.

Doing This For Me: Daily Healing

Date:

I Feel:

I Am Worthy Of:

Today I Will Stand Up For Myself By:

From Now On I Am:

Today I Plan To:

No More Excuses For/Towards:

Today I Will Invest In (Time, Money, Etc):

Everyday I Am Getting Better At:

Today's Compliment To Myself:

Today I Am Asking God For:

I Am Thanking God In Advance For:

I Am Not The Problem, But I Can Be The Solution.

Evening Thoughts

Today I Faced The Fear: _____.

I Am In Control Of Me.

Doing This For Me: Daily Healing

Date:

I Am Worthy Of:

From Now On I Am:

No More Excuses For/Towards:

Everyday I Am Getting Better At:

Today I Am Asking God For:

I Feel:

Today I Will Stand Up For Myself By:

Today I Plan To:

Today I Will Invest In (Time, Money, Etc):

Today's Compliment To Myself:

I Am Thanking God In Advance For:

I Am My Support Team.

Evening Thoughts

Today I Faced The Fear: _____.

Doing This For Me: Daily Healing

Date:

I Feel:

I Am Worthy Of:

Today I Will Stand Up For Myself By:

From Now On I Am:

Today I Plan To:

No More Excuses For/Towards:

Today I Will Invest In (Time, Money, Etc):

Everyday I Am Getting Better At:

Today's Compliment To Myself:

Today I Am Asking God For:

I Am Thanking God In Advance For:

I Am Learning How To Be There For Me.

Evening Thoughts

Today I Faced The Fear: _____.

Doing This For Me: Daily Healing

Date:

I Feel:

I Am Worthy Of:

Today I Will Stand Up For Myself By:

From Now On I Am:

Today I Plan To:

No More Excuses For/Towards:

Today I Will Invest In (Time, Money, Etc):

Everyday I Am Getting Better At:

Today's Compliment To Myself:

Today I Am Asking God For:

I Am Thanking God In Advance For:

It Is Okay For Me To Say Yes To Me.

Evening Thoughts

Today I Faced The Fear: _____.

Love Starts By Loving Myself. Every Step I Make To Protect And Invest In Myself Is My Way Of Pouring Love Into Me.

Made in the USA
Columbia, SC
17 March 2020